Artificial Intelligence and Ethics

Rizwan Raheem Ahmed, Ph.D.

DEDICATION

This book is dedicated to my Late Mother and Father who have provided me the financial, emotional, and Parental opportunities to raise me, provided higher education and supported me in my initial professional life journey.

TABLE OF CONTENTS

ACKNOWLEDGMENTS

I Acknowledge my wife who has supported me during writing this book. She has also helped me to generate book cover and other relevant material on Photoshop. She has encouraged me all the way in my journey.

INTRODUCTION

Artificial intelligence (AI) has emerged as a transformative force, revolutionizing industries and reshaping the way we live and interact with technology. From autonomous vehicles to personalized recommendations, AI systems are now deeply integrated into our daily lives. However, as AI becomes increasingly sophisticated and pervasive, it is crucial to examine the ethical implications that accompany its rapid advancement. The introduction sets the stage for the book by highlighting the significance of exploring the ethical dimensions of AI. It acknowledges the immense potential of AI to improve efficiency, productivity, and quality of life, but also recognizes the potential risks and challenges it poses. The introduction establishes the importance of responsible AI development, deployment, and decision-making that aligns with ethical principles.

The rise of artificial intelligence (AI) and its pervasive presence in modern society

The rise of artificial intelligence (AI) has ushered in a new era of technological advancements that are reshaping modern society. AI refers to the development of computer systems capable of performing tasks that typically require human intelligence, such as visual perception, speech recognition, decision-making, and problem-solving. With the exponential growth of data, computational power, and algorithmic advancements, AI has become increasingly sophisticated, leading to its pervasive presence in various aspects of our lives.

In today's society, AI systems are prevalent in numerous industries and sectors. From the moment, we wake up to the time we go to bed, we interact with AI in ways we may not always be aware of. AI powers voice assistants like Siri and Alexa, enabling us to control our smart homes and access information effortlessly. It underlies recommendation systems on streaming platforms like Netflix, suggesting personalized content based on our viewing habits and preferences. In e-commerce, AI algorithms analyze consumer behavior to provide targeted advertisements and product recommendations.

AI is also transforming healthcare. Machine learning algorithms assist in medical diagnoses, predict disease outcomes, and facilitate drug discovery. AI-powered robotic systems aid in surgical procedures, enhancing precision and minimizing human error. Moreover, AI applications are helping to tackle societal challenges, such as traffic management, environmental monitoring, and disaster response.

The rise of AI has not been limited to technological advancements alone; it has also had a profound impact on the economy and the job market. While AI automation has the potential to streamline processes, increase efficiency, and reduce costs, it also raises concerns about job displacement and the future of work. As AI systems continue to evolve, there is a need for re-skilling and upskilling the workforce to adapt to new roles and collaborate effectively with AI technologies.

However, the pervasive presence of AI also raises ethical considerations and challenges. As AI systems make decisions that affect individuals and society, questions of bias, fairness, transparency, accountability, and privacy emerge. The potential for unintended consequences, algorithmic biases, and the ethical implications of AI in sensitive domains like criminal justice and healthcare require careful examination and responsible AI development.

In conclusion, the rise of artificial intelligence has brought forth immense opportunities and challenges. AI's pervasive presence in modern society has transformed industries, improved efficiency, and enhanced our lives in various ways. However, the ethical implications and considerations associated with AI's widespread adoption necessitate ongoing dialogue, research, and responsible practices to ensure that AI aligns with human values and promotes the well-being of individuals and society as a whole.

Importance of exploring the ethical implications and considerations of AI

Exploring the ethical implications and considerations of artificial intelligence (AI) is of paramount importance for several compelling reasons:

Ensuring Human Well-being:

AI technologies have the potential to impact human lives in significant ways. From healthcare decisions to autonomous vehicles, AI systems have the capacity to make critical choices that directly influence human well-being. By thoroughly exploring the ethical implications, we can ensure that AI is designed and deployed in a manner that prioritizes human safety, health, and overall welfare.

Mitigating Bias and Discrimination:

AI systems are susceptible to inheriting biases from the data they are trained on. This can lead to discrimination and perpetuate societal inequalities. By exploring ethical considerations, we can develop approaches to address and mitigate bias, promoting fairness and equality in AI decision-making.

Safeguarding Privacy and Data Protection:

AI systems often rely on vast amounts of personal data to function effectively. It is crucial to examine the ethical dimensions of data collection, usage, and storage to protect individuals' privacy and prevent the misuse of sensitive information. Exploring these implications helps establish guidelines and safeguards to maintain data security and ensure responsible data practices.

Fostering Transparency and Accountability:

The inner workings of AI algorithms can be complex and opaque, making it challenging to understand the reasoning behind their decisions. By exploring the ethical considerations surrounding transparency and accountability, we can strive for AI systems that are explainable, auditable, and accountable for their actions. This enables individuals and organizations to trust and comprehend the decisions made by AI systems.

Promoting Social Acceptance and Trust:

Widespread acceptance and trust in AI technologies are crucial for their successful integration into society. By addressing ethical concerns and considering societal values, we can help build public trust in AI systems, leading to their responsible adoption and utilization for the greater good.

Anticipating and Mitigating Unintended Consequences:

The deployment of AI can have unforeseen consequences, both positive and negative. By exploring ethical implications, we can identify and anticipate potential risks and unintended outcomes. This proactive approach allows us to develop strategies to mitigate harm and maximize the positive impact of AI technologies.

Guiding Policy and Regulation:

Ethical considerations provide a foundation for

formulating policies and regulations that govern the development, deployment, and use of AI. By exploring these implications, policymakers can create frameworks that ensure ethical AI practices and protect societal interests.

In summary, exploring the ethical implications and considerations of AI is vital to guide responsible development, deployment, and utilization of AI technologies. By addressing these ethical dimensions, we can strive for AI systems that align with human values, promote fairness and transparency, safeguard privacy, and maximize the benefits while minimizing the risks associated with AI adoption.

Overview of the book's structure and objectives

The book aims to provide a comprehensive exploration of the ethical implications and considerations of artificial intelligence (AI). It delves into various dimensions of AI ethics, ranging from bias and fairness to privacy, transparency, accountability, and societal impact. The structure of the book is designed to systematically address these topics and foster a deeper understanding of the ethical challenges associated with AI.

Introduction:

The book begins with an introduction that highlights the rise of AI and its pervasive presence in modern society. It emphasizes the importance of exploring AI ethics and outlines the objectives of the book.

Understanding AI:

This chapter provides a foundational understanding of AI, its types, and key technologies behind it, such as machine learning and neural networks. It sets the stage for the subsequent ethical considerations.

Bias and Fairness:

The book explores the issue of bias in AI algorithms and datasets, emphasizing the ethical concerns surrounding biased decision-making. It discusses the importance of fairness in AI and explores strategies to mitigate bias and promote equitable outcomes.

Privacy and Data Protection:

This chapter examines the ethical considerations related to the collection, use, and storage of data in AI systems. It explores the importance of privacy and discusses approaches to protect personal data while leveraging AI technologies.

Transparency and Accountability:

The book explores the ethical dimensions of transparency and accountability in AI decision-making. It examines the challenges of understanding and explaining AI algorithms and outcomes, emphasizing the importance of accountable AI systems.

Societal Impact and Human Values:

This chapter delves into the broader societal impact of AI and its intersection with human values. It explores ethical considerations related to job displacement, social justice, cultural implications, and the need for AI to align with societal values.

Governance and Regulation:

The book discusses the role of governance and regulation in promoting ethical AI practices. It examines existing and emerging policies, frameworks, and international norms that guide AI development and deployment.

Ethical Frameworks and Decision-Making:

This chapter explores various ethical frameworks and principles that can guide AI decision-making. It examines the strengths and limitations of different ethical approaches and discusses their relevance in the context of AI ethics.

Future Perspectives and Ethical Progress:

The book concludes by reflecting on future perspectives in AI ethics and potential avenues for ethical progress. It encourages ongoing dialogue, interdisciplinary collaboration, and responsible AI development to shape a more ethically conscious AI landscape.

Throughout the book, real-world case studies, ethical dilemmas, and thought-provoking examples are presented to illustrate the practical application of ethical considerations in AI. The objective is to provide readers with a comprehensive understanding of AI ethics and equip them with the knowledge and insights to navigate the ethical challenges of AI in their own work and decision-making processes.

By addressing these topics and objectives, the book aims

to foster ethical awareness and responsible practices in AI development, deployment, and utilization, ensuring that AI technologies align with human values, promote fairness, and contribute positively to society.

CHAPTER 1: UNDERSTANDING ARTIFICIAL INTELLIGENCE

Definition and types of AI systems

Artificial Intelligence (AI) refers to the development and implementation of computer systems capable of performing tasks that typically require human intelligence. These systems aim to simulate human cognitive abilities, such as learning, problem-solving, perception, and decision-making.

There are various types of AI systems, each with its own characteristics and applications. Here are some common types of AI systems:

Narrow AI:

Also known as weak AI, narrow AI systems are designed

to perform specific tasks or functions. They are focused on solving well-defined problems within a limited domain. Examples include voice assistants like Siri or Alexa, recommendation systems, and image recognition algorithms.

General AI:

General AI refers to highly autonomous systems that possess human-level intelligence and can understand and perform any intellectual task that a human being can do. General AI systems have the ability to reason, learn, and adapt across multiple domains. However, achieving true general AI is still a hypothetical goal and has not been fully realized.

Machine Learning (ML):

Machine learning is a subset of AI that focuses on enabling systems to automatically learn and improve from experience without being explicitly programmed. ML algorithms learn from large datasets to identify patterns, make predictions, or perform specific tasks. It is commonly used in areas such as image recognition, natural language processing, and recommendation systems.

Deep Learning:

Deep learning is a subfield of machine learning that uses artificial neural networks to model and simulate the human brain's structure and function. Deep learning algorithms are capable of learning hierarchical representations of data, enabling them to process and analyze complex patterns. Deep learning has been successful in areas such as computer vision and natural language processing.

Reinforcement Learning:

Reinforcement learning involves training an AI system through interaction with an environment. The system learns to take actions to maximize rewards or minimize penalties based on feedback received from the environment. This approach is often used in applications such as robotics and game playing.

Expert Systems:

Expert systems are AI systems that emulate the decision-making ability of human experts in specific domains. They use rules and logic to provide expert-level recommendations or solutions based on a given set of inputs and knowledge.

Natural Language Processing (NLP):

NLP focuses on enabling computers to understand, interpret, and generate human language. NLP techniques are used in applications such as chatbots, language translation, sentiment analysis, and speech recognition.

It is important to note that these categories are not mutually exclusive, and AI systems can incorporate multiple approaches and techniques depending on their intended applications. The field of AI is continuously evolving, and researchers are constantly exploring new methods and technologies to advance the capabilities of AI systems.

Historical development and milestones in AI research

The field of Artificial Intelligence (AI) has a rich history of research and development, marked by several significant milestones. Here are some key historical developments in AI research:

Dartmouth Workshop (1956):

The Dartmouth Workshop, organized by John McCarthy, Marvin Minsky, Nathaniel Rochester, and Claude Shannon, is considered the birthplace of AI. The workshop brought together leading researchers to discuss and explore the potential of creating artificial intelligence.

Logic Theorist (1956):

Developed by Allen Newell and Herbert A. Simon, Logic Theorist became the first AI program capable of proving mathematical theorems.

General Problem Solver (1957):

Newell and Simon also developed the General Problem Solver, an AI program that could solve a wide range of problems using heuristics and problem-solving techniques.

Machine Learning (1950s-1960s):

Researchers such as Arthur Samuel and Frank Rosenblatt made significant contributions to the field of machine learning. Samuel's work on checkers-playing programs and Rosenblatt's development of the perceptron laid the foundation for machine learning algorithms.

ELIZA (1966):

ELIZA, developed by Joseph Weizenbaum, was an early natural language processing program that simulated a conversation by employing simple pattern matching techniques.

Expert Systems (1970s-1980s):

Expert systems emerged as a significant area of AI research during this period. MYCIN, developed by Edward Shortliffe, was a notable expert system capable of diagnosing and recommending treatments for bacterial infections.

The Fifth Generation Computer Systems Project (1982):

Initiated by the Japanese government, the Fifth Generation Computer Systems Project aimed to develop advanced AI and computer technologies. Although the project did not achieve all its goals, it led to advancements in areas such as parallel processing, logic programming, and distributed systems.

Deep Blue vs. Garry Kasparov (1997):

IBM's Deep Blue chess-playing computer defeated world chess champion Garry Kasparov in a historic match, showcasing the progress of AI in complex strategic decision-making.

Watson on Jeopardy! (2011):

IBM's Watson, a question-answering AI system, competed

on the game show Jeopardy! against human champions and emerged as the winner. This demonstrated the ability of AI systems to understand and respond to natural language questions.

AlphaGo vs. Lee Sedol (2016):

AlphaGo, developed by DeepMind, a subsidiary of Google, defeated world champion Go player Lee Sedol in a five-game match. Go had long been considered a challenging game for AI due to its complexity, making this a significant achievement.

These milestones represent some of the notable advancements in AI research. Since then, AI has continued to progress rapidly, with breakthroughs in areas such as deep learning, reinforcement learning, and the integration of AI into various domains and industries. Ongoing research and development continue to push the boundaries of AI capabilities and its impact on society.

Key components and technologies powering AI, including machine learning and neural networks

AI systems are powered by various components and technologies that enable them to perform intelligent tasks. Some key components and technologies driving AI include machine learning and neural networks.

Machine Learning (ML):

Machine learning is a subset of AI that focuses on the development of algorithms and models that allow systems to learn and improve from data without being explicitly programmed. ML algorithms enable AI systems to identify patterns, make predictions, and perform tasks based on data inputs. Some popular machine learning techniques include:

Supervised Learning:

In supervised learning, algorithms learn from labeled training data, where inputs are associated with corresponding desired outputs. The algorithms generalize from the training data to make predictions or classify new, unseen inputs accurately.

Unsupervised Learning:

Unsupervised learning algorithms learn from unlabeled data, aiming to discover hidden patterns or structures within the data. They are useful for tasks such as clustering and dimensionality reduction.

Reinforcement Learning:

Reinforcement learning involves training an AI agent through interactions with an environment. The agent receives rewards or penalties based on its actions, allowing it to learn optimal behaviors through trial and error.

Neural Networks:

Neural networks are a key technology within machine learning and AI. They are inspired by the structure and function of the human brain. Neural networks consist of interconnected nodes, called artificial neurons or units, organized in layers. Each neuron receives inputs, performs computations, and passes the output to the next layer.

Neural networks can learn from data by adjusting the weights and biases of the connections between neurons.

Deep Learning:

Deep learning is a subfield of machine learning that uses deep neural networks with multiple hidden layers. Deep learning has gained significant attention due to its ability to learn hierarchical representations of data, enabling it to excel in tasks such as image and speech recognition, natural language processing, and generative modeling.

Natural Language Processing (NLP):

NLP focuses on enabling computers to understand, interpret, and generate human language. It involves techniques for tasks such as sentiment analysis, language translation, speech recognition, and text generation. NLP technologies use machine learning, statistical models, and linguistic rules to process and understand text or speech data.

Computer Vision:

Computer vision involves the extraction, analysis, and interpretation of visual information from images or videos. It encompasses tasks such as object detection, image classification, facial recognition, and image segmentation. Deep learning techniques, particularly convolutional neural networks (CNNs), have significantly advanced the field of computer vision.

Robotics and Control Systems:

AI is employed in robotics and control systems to enable

machines to perceive, interact with, and respond to their environment. It involves techniques such as sensor fusion, path planning, localization, and manipulation. AI-powered robots and control systems are used in various domains, including manufacturing, healthcare, and autonomous vehicles.

These components and technologies form the foundation of AI systems, allowing them to learn, reason, and perform tasks that traditionally required human intelligence. The continuous advancement and integration of these technologies contribute to the rapid progress and real-world applications of AI in various fields.

CHAPTER 2: ETHICAL FRAMEWORKS FOR AI

Introduction to ethical theories and frameworks relevant to AI

When exploring the ethical implications of Artificial Intelligence (AI), it is important to consider various ethical theories and frameworks that provide guidance on how to assess the moral implications and decision-making processes related to AI development and deployment. Here are some of the prominent ethical theories and frameworks relevant to AI:

Utilitarianism:

Utilitarianism is a consequentialist ethical theory that focuses on maximizing overall happiness or utility. From a utilitarian perspective, AI systems should be designed and deployed in a way that maximizes societal welfare, considering the positive and negative impacts on individuals and communities. The ethical evaluation of AI would involve assessing the consequences and potential benefits or harms it may bring.

Deontology:

Deontology is an ethical theory that emphasizes the adherence to moral duties and principles. It emphasizes the inherent rights and intrinsic value of individuals. From a deontological perspective, AI systems should be designed and used in a way that respects human autonomy, dignity, and rights. Ethical evaluation would involve assessing whether the actions of AI systems respect moral principles, such as fairness, justice, and respect for persons.

Virtue Ethics:

Virtue ethics focuses on the development of virtuous character traits and moral values. It emphasizes the importance of cultivating virtues such as compassion, honesty, and fairness. In the context of AI, virtue ethics would involve considering the character traits and values exhibited in the development, deployment, and use of AI systems. Ethical evaluation would involve assessing whether AI promotes virtues and contributes to the overall moral character of society.

Rights-based Approaches:

Rights-based ethical frameworks emphasize the protection of individual rights and freedoms. In the context of AI, this involves considering the impact of AI systems on privacy, autonomy, freedom of expression, and other fundamental rights. Ethical evaluation would involve ensuring that AI respects and upholds individual rights, and any potential infringements are justified and necessary.

Ethical Pluralism:

Ethical pluralism recognizes that multiple ethical theories and principles may be relevant and applicable in different contexts. It acknowledges that no single theory can provide comprehensive answers to all ethical questions. Ethical evaluation within an ethical pluralistic framework would involve considering and balancing the principles and values from various ethical theories, recognizing the complexity and diversity of ethical considerations related to AI.

These ethical theories and frameworks provide different lenses through which to assess the ethical implications of AI. It is important to engage in ethical discussions and debates, considering these theories and frameworks, to ensure that AI development and deployment align with ethical principles and promote the well-being of individuals and society as a whole.

Examination of utilitarianism, deontology, virtue ethics, and other ethical approaches

Utilitarianism, deontology, virtue ethics, and other ethical approaches provide different perspectives and considerations when examining the ethical implications of Artificial Intelligence (AI). Let's delve into each of these approaches:

Utilitarianism:

Utilitarianism is a consequentialist ethical theory that focuses on maximizing overall happiness or utility. It assesses the morality of actions based on their outcomes. In the context of AI, utilitarianism would evaluate the consequences of AI systems in terms of their impact on societal welfare. It would consider factors such as the benefits AI brings, such as increased efficiency or improved quality of life, and weigh them against potential negative consequences, such as job displacement or privacy concerns. Utilitarianism aims to determine whether the overall net utility or happiness is maximized by the use of AI.

Deontology:

Deontology is an ethical theory that emphasizes the adherence to moral duties and principles. It focuses on the inherent rights and intrinsic value of individuals. From a deontological perspective, the moral evaluation of AI systems involves examining whether they respect and uphold moral principles, such as fairness, autonomy, and dignity. Deontologists would assess whether AI systems treat individuals as ends in themselves rather than as means to an end. This approach highlights the importance of ethical considerations regardless of the consequences or outcomes of AI.

Virtue Ethics:

Virtue ethics centers around developing virtuous character traits and moral values. It emphasizes cultivating virtues such as compassion, honesty, and fairness. In the context of AI, virtue ethics would focus on the character of individuals and the impact of AI on society's moral character. It evaluates whether AI systems promote virtues and contribute to the overall well-being of individuals and communities. Ethical assessment within a virtue ethics framework would involve considering whether AI aligns with virtuous values and fosters positive character development.

Rights-based Approaches:

Rights-based approaches prioritize the protection of individual rights and freedoms. They consider the inherent rights individuals possess and the moral obligations to respect those rights. In the context of AI, this involves assessing the impact of AI systems on privacy, autonomy, freedom of expression, and other fundamental rights. Ethical evaluation within a rights-based approach would involve ensuring that AI respects and upholds individual rights, and any potential infringements are justified and necessary.

Other ethical approaches, such as feminist ethics, care ethics, and communitarianism, also offer valuable perspectives on AI ethics. Feminist ethics examines issues of gender bias and equity, care ethics emphasizes empathy and care for individuals affected by AI systems, and communitarianism emphasizes the importance of community values and shared responsibilities.

In practice, ethical considerations often involve a combination of these approaches, as no single approach provides a comprehensive solution. Ethical discussions and debates informed by these different frameworks help ensure a well-rounded examination of AI's ethical implications and assist in making informed decisions that prioritize human well-being and societal values.

Applying ethical frameworks to AI development, deployment, and decision-making processes

Applying ethical frameworks to AI development, deployment, and decision-making processes is crucial for ensuring responsible and ethically sound practices. Here's how these frameworks can be applied:

Utilitarianism:

Utilitarianism's focus on maximizing overall happiness or utility can guide decision-making in AI. Developers and decision-makers can evaluate the potential benefits and harms of AI systems on different stakeholders. They can consider the consequences of AI deployment in terms of increased efficiency, improved services, or societal welfare, while also considering potential negative impacts such as job displacement or privacy concerns. Balancing these factors, the goal is to maximize the net utility or overall happiness.

Deontology:

Deontological ethics emphasizes adherence to moral duties and principles. When applying deontological principles to AI, developers and decision-makers can ensure that AI systems respect and uphold moral principles such as fairness, autonomy, and dignity. They can design AI systems that prioritize individual rights, privacy protection, and informed consent. Ethical considerations are based on whether the actions and behaviors of AI systems align with these moral principles.

Virtue Ethics:

Virtue ethics emphasizes cultivating virtuous character traits and moral values. Applying virtue ethics to AI involves developing AI systems that promote positive character traits and values. This includes designing AI systems that exhibit fairness, transparency, and empathy. Developers and decision-makers can foster a culture that encourages ethical behavior and responsible AI practices. They can also ensure that AI technologies contribute to the overall well-being of individuals and society by aligning with virtuous values.

Rights-based Approaches:

Rights-based approaches prioritize the protection of individual rights and freedoms. Applying this framework to AI involves respecting and upholding fundamental human rights in AI development and deployment. This includes ensuring privacy protection, avoiding discrimination, promoting freedom of expression, and providing avenues for redress in case of AI-related harms. Developers and decision-makers can conduct thorough impact assessments to identify potential rights implications and take necessary steps to protect and uphold those rights.

It is important to note that different ethical frameworks may lead to different ethical considerations and potential conflicts. Hence, a comprehensive and interdisciplinary approach that combines multiple ethical perspectives is often valuable. In practice, ethical decision-making involves engaging stakeholders, conducting ethical impact assessments, and adopting ethical guidelines and standards to ensure that AI is developed, deployed, and used responsibly and ethically. Ongoing dialogue, collaboration, and continuous ethical evaluation are essential for addressing emerging ethical challenges in the field of AI.

CHAPTER 3: BIAS AND FAIRNESS IN ARTIFICIAL INTELLIGENCE

The issue of bias in AI algorithms and datasets

The issue of bias in AI algorithms and datasets is a significant ethical concern in the field of AI. Bias refers to systematic errors or prejudices that are present in AI systems and can result in unfair or discriminatory outcomes. Bias can arise from various sources, including biased training data, biased algorithm design, or biased human decision-making that influences the AI system.

Biased Training Data:

AI algorithms learn from historical data, and if the training data is biased or reflects societal prejudices, the AI system can perpetuate and amplify those biases. For example, if a facial recognition algorithm is trained primarily on data of lighter-skinned individuals, it may have reduced accuracy in recognizing faces of darker-skinned individuals, leading to biased outcomes.

Biased Algorithm Design:

Bias can be introduced through the design and implementation of AI algorithms. Factors such as feature selection, algorithmic assumptions, and optimization objectives can inadvertently encode bias. If an algorithm is designed without considering the potential biases in the data or fails to account for the diversity of human experiences, it can result in discriminatory outcomes.

Biased Human Decision-Making:

Bias can also be introduced through human decision-making during the development and deployment of AI systems. Human biases, such as stereotypes or prejudices, can influence the decisions made in data collection, labeling, or algorithmic design, leading to biased AI systems.

The implications of bias in AI can be far-reaching and can result in unequal treatment, discrimination, or exclusion of certain groups. It can manifest in various domains, including criminal justice, hiring processes, loan approvals, and healthcare, exacerbating existing societal inequalities.

Addressing bias in AI requires proactive measures and considerations, including:

Diverse and Representative Data:

Ensuring that training data used to develop AI systems is diverse, representative, and free from biases is crucial. Data collection processes should include a wide range of individuals and demographic groups to mitigate underrepresentation and sampling biases.

Bias Detection and Mitigation:

Implementing mechanisms to detect and mitigate bias in AI algorithms is important. This can involve techniques such as data preprocessing, algorithmic fairness measures, and evaluation methods to identify and address biases.

Ethical Considerations:

Embedding ethical considerations and guidelines into the AI development process can help raise awareness of bias and encourage responsible practices. Ethical review boards, guidelines for data collection and usage, and diversity in AI teams can contribute to mitigating bias.

Transparency and Explainability:

Promoting transparency and explainability of AI systems can help uncover and understand biases. Users should be informed about the limitations, potential biases, and decision-making processes of AI algorithms to ensure accountability and allow for necessary checks and balances.

Addressing bias in AI requires a multidisciplinary approach involving collaboration between data scientists, domain experts, ethicists, and impacted communities. Continuous monitoring, evaluation, and improvement of AI systems are necessary to mitigate bias and promote fairness and equity in AI applications.

Understanding the concept of fairness and its challenges in AI

Fairness is a fundamental ethical principle that aims to ensure equitable treatment and equal opportunities for all individuals, regardless of their characteristics or attributes. In the context of AI, fairness refers to the absence of discriminatory or biased outcomes in the development, deployment, and use of AI systems. However, achieving fairness in AI presents several challenges:

Defining Fairness:

Fairness is a complex concept that can be interpreted and operationalized in different ways. There is no universally agreed-upon definition of fairness, and different stakeholders may have different perspectives on what constitutes fair outcomes. Different notions of fairness, such as equality, equity, or procedural fairness, may be applicable depending on the specific context and societal values.

Bias and Discrimination:

AI systems can inadvertently perpetuate biases and discrimination due to biased training data, algorithmic design, or decision-making processes. Identifying and addressing these biases is a challenging task, as biases can be subtle, implicit, or embedded in complex algorithms. Striking a balance between fairness and other objectives, such as accuracy or efficiency, can also be a challenge.

Trade-Offs and Conflicting Objectives:

Fairness often needs to be balanced with other considerations, such as accuracy, efficiency, or utility. In some cases, improving fairness may result in decreased accuracy or other performance metrics. Navigating these trade-offs requires careful consideration and understanding of the specific context and potential impacts on different stakeholders.

Group and Individual Fairness:

Determining fairness at the group level versus the individual level can be challenging. AI systems that optimize fairness at the group level may still exhibit disparities at the individual level, and vice versa. Resolving these tensions requires careful attention to the context and the potential impact on different subgroups or individuals within a population.

Representational Challenges:

Ensuring fairness in AI systems requires representative and unbiased data. However, obtaining such data can be challenging, as historical data often reflects existing societal biases and underrepresents certain groups. Addressing the representational challenges requires active efforts to mitigate bias in data collection and preprocessing stages.

Interpreting and Explainability:

Fairness in AI systems also involves the ability to interpret and explain the decision-making processes. Complex AI algorithms, such as deep neural networks, can be opaque and difficult to understand. Ensuring transparency and explainability of AI systems is essential for uncovering potential biases and building trust among users.

Addressing fairness challenges in AI requires a combination of technical solutions, ethical guidelines, and stakeholder engagement. It necessitates interdisciplinary collaboration involving AI researchers, ethicists, social scientists, policymakers, and impacted communities to develop robust and context-sensitive approaches to fairness in AI. Ongoing research, awareness, and dialogue are essential to navigate these challenges and ensure the responsible and equitable deployment of AI systems.

Mitigation strategies and techniques to address bias and promote fairness in AI systems

Mitigating bias and promoting fairness in AI systems is crucial to ensure ethical and equitable outcomes. Here are some strategies and techniques that can help address bias and promote fairness in AI:

Data Collection and Preprocessing:

Diverse and Representative Data: Collecting diverse and representative data that adequately represents the target population can help mitigate bias. This includes ensuring sufficient representation of various demographic groups and accounting for different social, cultural, and economic backgrounds.

Bias Detection and Correction: Implementing techniques to detect and correct biases in training data, such as statistical methods or data augmentation, can help minimize the impact of biased data on AI models.

Algorithmic Design and Development:

Fairness Measures: Incorporating fairness measures into the design of AI algorithms can help mitigate bias. For example, metrics like equalized odds or demographic parity can be used to assess and optimize fairness.

Regular Evaluation and Bias Monitoring: Continuously evaluating AI systems for bias and monitoring their performance across different subgroups can help identify and rectify any unintended biases that emerge over time.

Transparent and Explainable AI:

Interpretability and Explainability: Enhancing the transparency and interpretability of AI systems can help uncover biases and understand the factors contributing to decisions. Techniques such as rule-based models, interpretable machine learning, or model-agnostic explanation methods can aid in providing explanations for AI system outputs.

Bias Auditing and Reporting: Conducting bias audits and producing transparency reports that document the steps taken to address bias can enhance accountability and build trust among users.

Diversity and Interdisciplinary Collaboration:

Diverse Development Teams: Building diverse and inclusive teams that bring together individuals with different backgrounds, experiences, and perspectives can help identify and mitigate biases that might otherwise go unnoticed.

Interdisciplinary Collaboration: Encouraging collaboration between AI researchers, ethicists, social scientists, domain experts, and impacted communities can provide a more comprehensive understanding of biases and their societal implications.

Regular Ethical Reviews and Impact Assessments:

Ethical Review Boards: Establishing ethical review boards or committees that assess AI projects for potential biases and ethical concerns can help ensure the ethical development and deployment of AI systems.

Impact Assessments: Conducting regular impact assessments to identify and mitigate any adverse effects on individuals or communities' due to biases in AI systems.

Standards and Regulations:

Regulatory Frameworks: Developing and implementing regulatory frameworks and guidelines that address fairness and bias in AI can help set industry standards and ensure accountability. These frameworks can include requirements for bias detection and mitigation, transparency, and impact assessments.

It is important to note that no single solution can completely eliminate bias, as fairness is a complex and multifaceted challenge. Combining these strategies, along with ongoing research, learning from past experiences, and adapting to emerging ethical considerations, can contribute to the continuous improvement of fairness in AI systems.

CHAPTER 4: PRIVACY AND DATA PROTECTION

Ethical considerations surrounding the collection, use, and storage of data in AI

Ethical considerations surrounding the collection, use, and storage of data in AI are essential to protect individual privacy, ensure data security, and promote responsible AI practices. Here are some key ethical considerations in this regard:

Informed Consent:

Data Collection: Obtaining informed consent from individuals before collecting their data is crucial. Individuals should be informed about the purpose, scope, and potential risks associated with data collection, and they should have the right to control how their data is used.

Secondary Use of Data: If data collected for one purpose is to be used for other purposes, individuals should be informed and provided with an opportunity to give consent or opt out.

Privacy Protection:

Data Minimization: Collecting only the necessary data and minimizing the collection of sensitive or personally identifiable information (PII) can help protect individuals' privacy.

Anonymization and Pseudonymization: Implementing techniques to de-identify data, such as anonymization or pseudonymization, can reduce the risk of re-identification and protect individuals' privacy.

Data Security: Ensuring robust data security measures, including encryption, access controls, and secure storage, to prevent unauthorized access, breaches, or misuse of personal data.

Transparency and Accountability:

Data Usage Policies: Clearly communicating the purposes, scope, and potential recipients of data to individuals can promote transparency and enable them to make informed decisions.

Accountability: Assigning responsibility to data controllers and processors to handle data ethically and securely. This includes establishing mechanisms for individuals to exercise their rights, such as access, rectification, and deletion of their data.

Fairness and Avoidance of Discrimination:

Bias Mitigation: Taking measures to detect and address biases in data collection, preprocessing, and algorithmic design to avoid unfair or discriminatory outcomes.

Equity in Data Representation: Ensuring diverse and representative data to avoid underrepresentation or marginalization of certain groups, which can lead to biased AI systems.

Data Governance and Regulation:

Compliance with Legal and Regulatory Requirements: Adhering to applicable data protection laws and regulations to safeguard individuals' rights and protect their personal data.

Ethical Guidelines: Developing and adhering to ethical guidelines and standards for data collection, use, and storage in AI systems. These guidelines can provide principles for responsible data practices and promote ethical decision-making.

Data Lifecycles and Retention:

Data Retention: Establishing clear policies for data retention and ensuring that data is retained only for as long as necessary, minimizing the risk of unauthorized access or misuse.

Data Disposal: Properly disposing of data once it is no

longer required, using secure deletion methods or anonymization techniques to protect individuals' privacy.

Considering these ethical considerations in the collection, use, and storage of data in AI systems helps protect individuals' privacy, maintain trust, and promote responsible and ethical AI practices. Engaging in ongoing dialogue, incorporating diverse perspectives, and adhering to evolving ethical standards are essential for addressing emerging ethical challenges in data-driven AI applications.

Exploration of privacy concerns and the potential risks of data misuse

Privacy concerns and the potential risks of data misuse are significant ethical considerations in the context of AI. Here are some key aspects to explore:

Unauthorized Access and Data Breaches:

Data Security: Inadequate security measures or vulnerabilities in AI systems can lead to unauthorized access, data breaches, or cyberattacks. This can result in sensitive personal information being exposed or misused by malicious actors.

Profiling and Surveillance:

Profiling: AI systems that analyze and process large amounts of data can create detailed profiles of individuals, including their behaviors, preferences, and characteristics. Profiling can lead to privacy invasions, as individuals may have limited control over how their data is used to make decisions or target them with personalized advertisements.

Surveillance: Widespread deployment of AI-powered surveillance systems, such as facial recognition or tracking technologies, raises concerns about the erosion of privacy and the potential for constant monitoring of individuals' activities.

Secondary Use and Data Sharing:

Data Monetization: Personal data collected by AI systems may be used for purposes beyond the original intent of data collection, such as targeted advertising or selling to third parties. Individuals may have limited awareness or control over how their data is shared or monetized.

Data Aggregation: Aggregating data from multiple sources can lead to the creation of comprehensive profiles and raise privacy concerns. Data sharing between organizations or across borders can further exacerbate these risks.

Re-identification and De-anonymization:

Re-identification Attacks: Anonymized or pseudonymized data can still carry privacy risks, as it may be possible to re-identify individuals by linking different datasets or using other external information.

Machine Learning and Inference Attacks: AI systems trained on large datasets can sometimes reveal sensitive information unintentionally through machine learning or inference attacks. For example, statistical analysis of aggregated data may inadvertently disclose personal attributes.

Contextual Privacy and Data Sensitivity:

Contextual Privacy: Respecting individuals' contextual privacy involves considering the specific context and sensitivity of the data being collected. Data that may seem harmless in isolation can become intrusive when combined with other data or used in certain contexts.

Sensitive Personal Data: The collection and use of sensitive personal data, such as health information or biometric data, raise additional privacy concerns due to the heightened risk of harm or discrimination if mishandled or misused.

Lack of Control and Informed Consent:

Lack of Control: Individuals may have limited control over their personal data once it is collected by AI systems. They may not be aware of how their data is used, shared, or stored, leading to a loss of autonomy.

Informed Consent: Obtaining informed consent from individuals is crucial for ensuring privacy. However, complexities in AI systems, opaque algorithms, or lengthy privacy policies may hinder individuals' ability to make informed decisions about their data.

Addressing privacy concerns and mitigating the risks of data misuse require proactive measures and ethical safeguards. This includes implementing robust data protection practices, ensuring transparency and user control over data usage, adopting privacy-enhancing technologies, and adhering to legal and regulatory frameworks for data privacy and security. It is important for organizations, policymakers, and AI developers to prioritize privacy protection and empower individuals with rights and control over their personal data to build trust and uphold ethical standards in AI applications.

Legal and regulatory frameworks for protecting privacy in the context of AI

Legal and regulatory frameworks play a crucial role in protecting privacy in the context of AI. Here are some key legal and regulatory considerations for privacy protection:

General Data Protection Regulation (GDPR):

The GDPR, implemented in the European Union (EU), sets comprehensive regulations for data protection and privacy. It establishes principles, rights, and obligations for organizations handling personal data, including AI systems. The GDPR includes requirements such as informed consent, data minimization, purpose limitation, and the right to access and rectify personal data.

California Consumer Privacy Act (CCPA):

The CCPA is a landmark privacy law in California, United States, which grants consumers certain rights regarding the collection, use, and sale of their personal information. It requires businesses to provide clear notices, obtain consent, and offer opt-out mechanisms to protect consumer privacy.

Personal Information Protection and Electronic Documents Act (PIPEDA):

PIPEDA is a Canadian federal law governing the

collection, use, and disclosure of personal information by private sector organizations. It outlines principles for consent, accountability, transparency, and individual rights in relation to personal data.

Artificial Intelligence Act (AIA):

Proposed by the European Commission, the AIA aims to regulate AI systems, including their impact on fundamental rights and data protection. It includes provisions related to high-risk AI applications, transparency, accountability, and conformity assessment.

Sector-Specific Regulations:

Various industries and sectors have specific regulations for privacy and data protection. For example, the Health Insurance Portability and Accountability Act (HIPAA) in the healthcare sector and the Payment Card Industry Data Security Standard (PCI DSS) for the payment card industry provide specific requirements for safeguarding personal data.

International Data Transfer Mechanisms:

Cross-border data transfers require adequate safeguards to protect personal data. Mechanisms such as Standard Contractual Clauses (SCCs), Binding Corporate Rules (BCRs), and the EU-U.S. Privacy Shield (for EU-U.S. transfers) provide legal frameworks for ensuring privacy when transferring data across jurisdictions.

Regulatory Agencies and Authorities:

Privacy and data protection authorities, such as the

Information Commissioner's Office (ICO) in the UK, the Federal Trade Commission (FTC) in the US, and the Data Protection Commission (DPC) in Ireland, enforce and interpret privacy laws, investigate violations, and provide guidance on privacy best practices.

Ethical Guidelines and Principles:

Alongside legal frameworks, ethical guidelines and principles for AI development and deployment may address privacy concerns. For instance, the OECD AI Principles, the IEEE Ethically Aligned Design, and the AI Ethics Guidelines by various organizations provide guidance on privacy protection, transparency, and accountability.

It is important for organizations to comply with applicable legal frameworks, engage in privacy impact assessments, adopt privacy by design principles, and establish robust data governance practices. Regular updates and adaptation of legal and regulatory frameworks are essential to keep pace with emerging technologies and evolving privacy risks associated with AI.

CHAPTER 5: ACCOUNTABILITY AND TRANSPARENCY

The importance of accountability in AI decision-making

Accountability in AI decision-making is of paramount importance for several reasons:

Transparency and Explainability:

AI systems often operate with complex algorithms and models that may be difficult to understand or interpret. Accountability ensures that the decision-making process is transparent and explainable, allowing stakeholders to understand why specific decisions were made and how they were reached. This transparency helps build trust in AI systems and facilitates effective oversight.

Detecting and Addressing Biases:

AI systems can inadvertently perpetuate biases present in the data they are trained on or the algorithms they utilize. Accountability holds organizations responsible for detecting and addressing biases in AI decision-making, ensuring fairness and preventing discriminatory outcomes.

Legal and Ethical Compliance:

Accountability ensures that AI systems and their decision-making processes comply with legal and ethical standards. It holds organizations liable for any violations of laws, regulations, or ethical guidelines, promoting responsible and lawful use of AI technologies.

Mitigating Harms and Negative Impacts:

AI systems have the potential to impact individuals and society in significant ways. Accountability ensures that AI developers and deployers consider the potential harms and negative impacts of AI decision-making and take necessary measures to mitigate them. It encourages the responsible use of AI, minimizing risks to individuals' rights, well-being, and safety.

Oversight and Governance:

Accountability provides a framework for effective oversight and governance of AI systems. It establishes mechanisms for monitoring the performance, behavior, and impact of AI systems, enabling corrective actions to be taken when necessary.

Trust and Social Acceptance:

Accountability contributes to building trust in AI systems among users, stakeholders, and the broader public. When organizations are accountable for their AI decision-making, it instills confidence that the systems are being used in a responsible and ethical manner, fostering social acceptance and adoption.

To ensure accountability in AI decision-making, organizations should establish clear lines of responsibility, define roles and obligations, and implement mechanisms for audits, transparency, and independent reviews. This includes documenting the decision-making process, monitoring the system's behavior, and providing avenues for feedback and redress. Additionally, regulatory frameworks and industry standards can play a crucial role in enforcing accountability and incentivizing responsible AI practices.

Challenges in understanding and explaining AI algorithms and outcomes

Understanding and explaining AI algorithms and outcomes present several challenges, including the following:

Algorithmic Complexity:

AI algorithms can be highly complex, involving intricate mathematical models and computations. They often operate in high-dimensional spaces and utilize advanced techniques such as deep learning or reinforcement learning. The complexity of these algorithms can make it difficult for non-experts to comprehend their inner workings and understand how they arrive at specific decisions or predictions.

Lack of Transparency:

Some AI algorithms, such as deep neural networks, are characterized by their black-box nature, meaning that it is challenging to trace the specific factors or features that influence their outputs. The lack of transparency hinders understanding and makes it challenging to explain the reasoning behind AI decisions.

Data Bias and Unintended Consequences:

AI algorithms are trained on vast amounts of data, which can introduce biases or reflect societal inequalities present in the data. Unintended consequences may arise from biased training data or algorithmic biases, leading to unfair or discriminatory outcomes. Explaining the decisions made by biased algorithms can be challenging and may require careful examination of the underlying data and decision-making processes.

Dynamic and Evolving Systems:

AI algorithms can continuously learn and adapt to new data, leading to dynamic and evolving systems. The outcomes produced by these algorithms may change over time, making it challenging to provide a static or fixed explanation for their behavior.

Lack of Standardization:

There is currently no standardized approach to explain AI algorithms and their outcomes. Different AI models and techniques may require different explanation methods, and there is ongoing research and development in the field of explainable AI (XAI) to address this challenge. The lack of standardization can make it difficult to compare and evaluate different AI systems or to provide consistent explanations across diverse AI applications.

Complexity-Interpretability Trade-off:

There is often a trade-off between the complexity of an AI algorithm and its interpretability. As AI algorithms become more complex and powerful, they may sacrifice interpretability. Simpler models, such as decision trees or linear regression, are more interpretable but may have limitations in terms of their predictive performance. Striking a balance between complexity and interpretability is a challenge in designing and explaining AI algorithms.

Addressing these challenges requires research and development in the field of XAI, which aims to develop methods and techniques to make AI algorithms more understandable and explainable. It involves creating interpretable models, developing post-hoc explanation techniques, and establishing evaluation criteria for explainability. Standardization efforts and interdisciplinary collaborations involving experts in AI, ethics, psychology, and law can contribute to advancing the understanding and explainability of AI algorithms and outcomes.

Ethical guidelines for ensuring transparency in AI systems and algorithms

Ethical guidelines for ensuring transparency in AI systems and algorithms play a crucial role in promoting responsible and accountable AI practices. Here are some key ethical considerations and guidelines:

Explainability and Interpretability:

AI systems should strive to be explainable and provide meaningful explanations for their decisions and actions. The guidelines should emphasize the importance of clear and understandable explanations that can be communicated to users, stakeholders, and affected individuals.

Transparency should be promoted through the use of interpretable algorithms and models, allowing users to understand how the system arrives at its conclusions and enabling them to trust and verify the outcomes.

Disclosure of AI Use:

Organizations deploying AI systems should be transparent about their use of AI and clearly communicate when AI algorithms are involved in decision-making processes that impact individuals. This ensures that users and stakeholders are aware of the presence of AI and can make informed decisions.

Data Collection and Use:

Ethical guidelines should emphasize transparency regarding data collection and use. Organizations should be transparent about the types of data being collected, the purposes for which they are collected, and how they will be used in AI systems. Users should have clear visibility and control over their data.

Risk Assessment and Mitigation:

Ethical guidelines should require organizations to conduct

risk assessments to identify potential biases, discrimination, or adverse impacts that may result from AI systems. Transparently documenting these assessments and implementing strategies to mitigate risks are essential.

Human Oversight and Accountability:

Ethical guidelines should advocate for human oversight in AI decision-making processes, particularly in high-stakes domains. There should be mechanisms in place to review and challenge the outcomes of AI systems, with human intervention where necessary. Accountability for AI systems' decisions and actions should be clearly assigned.

Openness and Collaboration:

Guidelines should encourage openness and collaboration in the AI community. This involves sharing knowledge, methodologies, and best practices related to transparency. Collaborative efforts can help identify common challenges, develop standards, and improve transparency across the field.

User Empowerment:

Ethical guidelines should prioritize empowering users by providing them with understandable and accessible information about AI systems. Users should have the ability to make informed decisions, understand how their data is used, and have control over their interactions with AI systems.

Continuous Monitoring and Auditing:

Ethical guidelines should emphasize the importance of

ongoing monitoring and auditing of AI systems to ensure transparency. Regular assessments should be conducted to evaluate the performance, fairness, and transparency of AI algorithms. This helps identify and rectify any issues that may arise during the system's lifecycle.

It is crucial for organizations, policymakers, and AI practitioners to adopt and adhere to these ethical guidelines to ensure transparency in AI systems and algorithms. They contribute to building trust, promoting accountability, and mitigating the potential risks and harms associated with AI technologies.

CHAPTER 6: AUTONOMOUS SYSTEMS AND MORAL AGENCY

Examining the ethical dimensions of autonomous systems and their decision-making capabilities

Examining the ethical dimensions of autonomous systems and their decision-making capabilities raises important considerations and challenges. Here are some key ethical dimensions to explore:

Accountability and Responsibility:

Autonomous systems, such as self-driving cars or robots, can make decisions and take actions without direct human intervention. The ethical question arises as to who should be held accountable when autonomous systems make decisions that result in harm or have unintended consequences. Determining responsibility and allocating liability is a complex issue that requires careful consideration.

Transparency and Explainability:

Autonomous systems often operate using complex algorithms and models, making it challenging to understand their decision-making process. Ethical concerns arise when autonomous systems produce outcomes that are difficult to explain or when they exhibit "black-box" behavior. The lack of transparency and explainability can hinder trust, oversight, and the ability to address biases or discriminatory behavior.

Value Alignment and Ethical Priorities:

Autonomous systems need to align with ethical principles and societal values. Determining the ethical priorities and value trade-offs of autonomous systems is critical. For example, a self-driving car might face a situation where it has to make a split-second decision that could potentially harm either the passengers or pedestrians. Deciding the ethical guidelines and priorities for such situations is a complex and value-laden task.

Unforeseen Consequences and Adaptability:

Autonomous systems may encounter situations or environments that were not explicitly anticipated during their development or training. Ethical considerations arise when autonomous systems need to adapt to novel scenarios and make decisions with potential ethical implications. Balancing adaptability with ensuring adherence to ethical principles can be challenging.

Equity and Distribution of Benefits:

Autonomous systems can have wide-ranging impacts on society, including economic, social, and environmental consequences. Ethical concerns arise when these systems exacerbate existing inequalities or fail to distribute the benefits and risks fairly. Ensuring equitable access, benefits, and addressing potential biases in autonomous systems is crucial for ethical decision-making.

Human Autonomy and Control:

The degree of human autonomy and control in autonomous systems raises ethical questions. There is a need to strike a balance between human decision-making and the automation capabilities of autonomous systems. Ethical considerations include preserving human agency, providing overrides, and addressing concerns about loss of control or excessive reliance on autonomous technologies.

Long-term Effects and Unintended Harms:

Ethical dimensions also encompass the long-term effects and unintended harms that can result from the widespread deployment of autonomous systems. Evaluating the societal impacts, such as job displacement, economic inequalities, or unintended consequences on human behavior, is essential for responsible and ethical implementation.

Examining these ethical dimensions involves interdisciplinary collaboration, engaging stakeholders, and developing frameworks and guidelines for the responsible design, development, and deployment of autonomous systems. It requires addressing technical challenges alongside ethical considerations to ensure that autonomous systems align with societal values, promote human well-being, and contribute positively to society.

The concept of moral agency and responsibility in AI systems

The concept of moral agency and responsibility in AI systems raises important questions regarding the ethical implications of their actions and the allocation of responsibility. Here are key considerations:

Moral Agency of AI Systems:

Moral agency refers to the capacity to make moral judgments and be held morally responsible for one's actions. Traditional notions of moral agency as applied to humans may not directly translate to AI systems. AI systems lack consciousness, intentionality, and subjective experience, which are foundational to human moral agency.

Proximate and Ultimate Responsibility:

While AI systems may not possess moral agency in the same way humans do, responsibility can still be assigned to different stakeholders involved in their design, development, and deployment. Proximate responsibility lies with the individuals and organizations responsible for creating and deploying AI systems. They are accountable for ensuring the systems are designed ethically, trained on unbiased data, and adhere to legal and ethical guidelines.

Ultimate responsibility lies with the human decision-makers who determine the goals, objectives, and constraints of the AI systems. They are responsible for the choices made during the development and deployment process.

Human Oversight and Control:

Humans play a critical role in the ethical use of AI systems. They are responsible for monitoring, overseeing, and maintaining control over the decisions and actions of AI systems.

Ethical considerations include establishing mechanisms for human intervention, providing avenues for human review and override, and ensuring that AI systems do not operate beyond human-defined boundaries.

Designing Ethical Frameworks:

Building ethical frameworks and guidelines for AI systems can help establish responsible behavior and accountability. These frameworks should incorporate considerations of fairness, transparency, accountability, privacy, and other ethical principles.

Designers and developers should strive to embed ethical decision-making processes into the development and deployment of AI systems, enabling them to align with societal values and ethical standards.

Human Values and Value Alignment:

AI systems should reflect and align with human values. This requires integrating societal norms, ethical principles, and cultural considerations into the design and decision-making processes.

Ethical challenges arise when AI systems encounter situations where values conflict or require trade-offs. Determining the appropriate values and priorities to guide AI systems' actions is a complex ethical task.

Continuous Monitoring and Iterative Improvement:

Ethical responsibility involves ongoing monitoring, evaluation, and improvement of AI systems. Regular audits, transparency reports, and accountability mechanisms are crucial for identifying and rectifying biases, unintended consequences, or ethical issues that arise during the system's lifecycle.

Legal and Regulatory Frameworks:

Governments and regulatory bodies play a role in defining the legal and regulatory frameworks that govern AI systems. These frameworks help establish the legal responsibilities of different stakeholders and provide guidelines for ethical behavior and accountability.

Navigating the concept of moral agency and responsibility in AI systems requires interdisciplinary dialogue involving ethicists, AI researchers, policymakers, and society at large. It involves carefully considering the impact of AI systems, promoting human oversight, and developing ethical frameworks that ensure AI systems align with societal values and promote the overall well-being of individuals and communities.

Ethical dilemmas and considerations in designing and deploying autonomous AI technologies

Designing and deploying autonomous AI technologies presents various ethical dilemmas and considerations. Here are some key points to explore:

Safety and Risk:

Ensuring the safety of autonomous AI technologies is crucial. Ethical considerations involve minimizing the risk of harm to humans, both directly and indirectly. Striking the right balance between innovation and safety is a challenge, particularly in high-stakes domains such as autonomous vehicles or healthcare.

Ethical Decision-Making:

Autonomous AI technologies may encounter situations that require ethical decision-making. Ethical considerations arise when determining how AI systems should prioritize values, resolve conflicts, and make choices that align with societal norms and ethical principles. Deciding on the appropriate ethical frameworks and guidelines for these decisions is complex.

Bias and Discrimination:

Bias in AI systems can perpetuate existing societal inequalities and lead to discriminatory outcomes. Ethical dilemmas arise when autonomous AI technologies reflect and amplify biases present in training data or algorithms.

Addressing bias and promoting fairness require careful consideration of data collection, algorithmic design, and ongoing monitoring.

Privacy and Data Protection:

Autonomous AI technologies often rely on collecting and analyzing vast amounts of personal data. Ethical considerations involve ensuring individuals' privacy rights are respected, obtaining informed consent, and protecting sensitive information from unauthorized access or misuse. Striking a balance between data-driven innovation and privacy preservation is critical.

Transparency and Explainability:

The lack of transparency and explainability in autonomous AI technologies can raise ethical concerns. Individuals impacted by AI systems may have a right to understand the reasoning behind decisions that affect them. Ethical dilemmas arise when trade-offs are made between explainability and performance, as well as addressing proprietary concerns.

Unintended Consequences:

The deployment of autonomous AI technologies can have unintended consequences. Ethical considerations involve anticipating and mitigating potential negative impacts on employment, social dynamics, and human behavior. Balancing the benefits of AI technologies with the potential harms and unintended consequences is an ongoing ethical dilemma.

Social and Economic Disruption:

Autonomous AI technologies have the potential to disrupt industries, economies, and job markets. Ethical dilemmas arise in addressing the social and economic implications of job displacement, ensuring a just transition for affected individuals, and minimizing inequalities that may result from AI-driven automation.

Human-Computer Interaction and User Experience:

Ethical considerations include designing autonomous AI technologies that provide a positive user experience and foster trust. Ensuring that users understand the capabilities, limitations, and potential risks of AI technologies is crucial. Ethical dilemmas arise when balancing the desire for seamless automation with maintaining human control and engagement.

Long-term Effects and Accountability:

Deploying autonomous AI technologies may have long-term effects on society and future generations. Ethical dilemmas involve considering the potential consequences, unintended uses, and accountability for the long-term impacts of AI systems. Establishing mechanisms for ongoing evaluation, responsibility, and accountability is critical.

Navigating these ethical dilemmas and considerations requires a multidisciplinary approach, involving experts in ethics, AI, law, and social sciences. It involves transparent and inclusive decision-making processes that consider a broad range of perspectives and prioritize the well-being and values of individuals and society as a whole.

CHAPTER 7: AI AND HUMAN LABOR

Impacts of AI on employment and the future of work

The impacts of AI on employment and the future of work are significant and raise several ethical considerations. Here are key points to explore:

Job Displacement and Automation:

AI has the potential to automate various tasks and jobs, leading to job displacement in certain sectors. This raises ethical dilemmas regarding the impact on individuals who lose their livelihoods and face challenges in finding new employment opportunities.

Skill Requirements and Job Transformation:

AI technologies may change the skill requirements for the

workforce. While some jobs may be eliminated, new jobs that leverage AI capabilities may emerge. Ethical considerations involve ensuring access to upskilling and reskilling opportunities, ensuring a just transition for affected workers, and addressing potential inequalities in access to these opportunities.

Economic Inequalities and Distribution of Benefits:

The adoption of AI technologies can exacerbate existing economic inequalities. Ethical concerns arise when the benefits of AI-driven productivity gains are unevenly distributed, concentrating wealth and power in certain segments of society. Ensuring equitable distribution of benefits and addressing potential disparities is essential.

Human-AI Collaboration and Augmentation:

Ethical considerations involve exploring the potential for human-AI collaboration and augmentation. Rather than outright job replacement, AI technologies can be designed to enhance human capabilities, enabling individuals to focus on tasks that require creativity, critical thinking, and empathy. Ensuring that AI systems are designed to support human well-being and job satisfaction is crucial.

Worker Surveillance and Privacy:

The implementation of AI technologies in workplaces can raise concerns about worker surveillance and privacy. Ethical considerations involve striking a balance between utilizing AI for monitoring and efficiency purposes while respecting worker privacy rights. Transparency, informed consent, and clear policies on data collection and usage are crucial in protecting worker privacy.

Algorithmic Bias and Discrimination:

AI systems can inherit biases from the data on which they are trained, potentially leading to discriminatory outcomes. Ethical dilemmas arise when biases in AI algorithms impact hiring decisions, performance evaluations, or access to opportunities. Addressing algorithmic bias and ensuring fairness in AI-driven employment processes are important considerations.

Human Dignity and Meaningful Work:

The rise of AI raises questions about the impact on human dignity and the nature of meaningful work. Ethical considerations involve ensuring that AI technologies are designed and deployed in ways that preserve human dignity, value human contribution, and provide opportunities for individuals to engage in work that aligns with their skills and aspirations.

Social and Economic Disruption:

The widespread adoption of AI technologies may lead to broader social and economic disruptions. Ethical considerations involve managing the potential negative consequences, such as inequality, unemployment, and societal upheaval. Policies and initiatives that address the social and economic impacts of AI are essential.

Addressing the impacts of AI on employment and the future of work requires a proactive approach that combines ethical considerations, policy interventions, and a focus on human well-being. This involves collaboration between governments, businesses, educational institutions, and society as a whole to ensure a just and inclusive transition to a future where AI technologies enhance human potential and contribute to overall societal welfare.

Ethical considerations regarding job displacement and re-skilling

Ethical considerations regarding job displacement and re-skilling in the context of AI-driven automation are crucial. Here are key points to explore:

Fairness and Social Justice:

Ethical concerns arise when job displacement disproportionately affects certain individuals or communities, exacerbating existing social inequalities. Ensuring fairness in the distribution of the burdens and benefits of AI-driven automation is essential. Policies and initiatives should be designed to minimize the negative impacts on vulnerable populations and provide equitable opportunities for re-skilling and job transition.

Access to Reskilling and Upskilling:

Ethical considerations involve ensuring that individuals affected by job displacement have access to quality reskilling and upskilling opportunities. This includes providing resources, training programs, and educational support to facilitate the transition into new industries or occupations. Accessible and affordable re-skilling initiatives should be prioritized to prevent individuals from being left behind.

Worker Empowerment and Agency:

Ethical considerations involve empowering workers to actively participate in decisions related to their re-skilling and career transitions. Workers should have a voice in shaping policies, training programs, and the design of AI technologies that impact their employment. Ensuring worker agency promotes dignity, autonomy, and a sense of control over one's professional trajectory.

Continuous Learning and Lifelong Education:

Ethical considerations extend beyond immediate re-skilling efforts to support lifelong learning. The rapid pace of technological advancements demands continuous learning and adaptability. Ethical obligations include creating a culture that encourages lifelong education, providing access to learning resources, and promoting a mindset of personal and professional growth.

Worker Support and Social Safety Nets:

Ethical considerations involve providing adequate support for workers who face job displacement. Social safety nets, such as unemployment benefits, healthcare, and income support, should be in place to cushion the impact of job loss and ensure individuals have a dignified standard of living during their transition period. Offering financial assistance, counseling services, and job placement assistance can help ease the challenges of re-skilling and job search.

Mitigating Psychological and Emotional Impact:

Ethical considerations include recognizing and addressing the psychological and emotional impact of job displacement. Losing a job can lead to feelings of insecurity, anxiety, and a loss of identity. Providing emotional support, counseling, and mental health resources can help individuals navigate the emotional challenges associated with career transitions.

Anticipating Future Disruptions:

Ethical considerations involve anticipating and preparing for future disruptions in the labor market. Proactive planning and investment in anticipating skills needs, identifying emerging industries, and fostering a culture of innovation can help individuals adapt to changing job demands. Governments, businesses, and educational institutions should collaborate to align re-skilling efforts with future labor market requirements.

Addressing the ethical considerations related to job displacement and re-skilling requires a multi-stakeholder approach involving governments, businesses, educational institutions, labor unions, and civil society organizations. By prioritizing fairness, worker empowerment, continuous learning, and comprehensive support systems, society can strive for a just and inclusive transition in the face of AI-driven automation.

Potential solutions and policies to address the social and economic consequences of AI-driven automation

Addressing the social and economic consequences of AI-driven automation requires a comprehensive approach involving various solutions and policies. Here are key potential solutions and policies to consider:

Education and Skill Development:

Investing in education and skill development programs that focus on emerging fields, technology literacy, and critical thinking skills. This includes fostering collaborations between educational institutions, industry, and government to ensure that the workforce is equipped with the skills needed for the jobs of the future.

Lifelong Learning Initiatives:

Promoting a culture of lifelong learning and continuous upskilling. Encouraging individuals to embrace learning opportunities throughout their careers and providing accessible resources, such as online courses, vocational training programs, and mentorship opportunities.

Job Transition Support:

Developing robust support systems to assist individuals in transitioning to new careers. This includes providing job placement services, career counseling, and financial support during the transition period. Governments and organizations can establish retraining programs and collaborate with industries to facilitate smooth job transitions.

Universal Basic Income (UBI):

Exploring the concept of a universal basic income, which provides a guaranteed income to all individuals regardless of employment status. UBI can act as a safety net, ensuring a basic standard of living and providing individuals with the freedom to pursue re-skilling, entrepreneurship, or other meaningful activities.

Labor Market Regulations:

Evaluating and adapting labor market regulations to accommodate the changing nature of work. This may include exploring new employment models, such as flexible work arrangements, job-sharing, and gig economy regulations, to provide individuals with more opportunities for income generation and job security.

Social Safety Nets:

Strengthening social safety nets to support individuals affected by job displacement. Enhancing unemployment benefits, healthcare coverage, and social assistance programs can provide temporary relief and ensure a dignified standard of living during the transition period.

Public-Private Partnerships:

Encouraging collaboration between the public and private sectors to address the social and economic consequences of AI-driven automation. Governments, businesses, and civil society organizations can work together to identify potential challenges, develop innovative solutions, and implement policies that promote inclusive growth and equitable distribution of benefits.

Ethical Guidelines and Regulations:

Establishing ethical guidelines and regulations to govern the development and deployment of AI technologies.

These guidelines can ensure that AI systems are designed to prioritize human well-being, fairness, transparency, and accountability. Regulations can address issues such as data privacy, algorithmic bias, and the responsible use of AI in various domains.

Support for Entrepreneurship and Innovation:

Fostering an environment that supports entrepreneurship and innovation. Encouraging the creation of new businesses, startups, and innovation hubs can generate job opportunities and drive economic growth. Providing resources, mentorship, and access to capital can help individuals harness the potential of AI technologies for their entrepreneurial endeavors.

International Cooperation:

Encouraging international cooperation and collaboration to address the global impacts of AI-driven automation. Sharing best practices, knowledge, and resources among countries can facilitate the development of comprehensive policies that mitigate negative consequences and promote positive outcomes on a global scale.

Implementing these solutions and policies requires a holistic approach that balances the benefits of AI-driven automation with the well-being of individuals and society as a whole. It requires collaboration among governments, businesses, educational institutions, labor unions, and civil society organizations to create a sustainable and inclusive future of work in the age of AI.

CHAPTER 8: AI AND SOCIAL JUSTICE

Exploring the intersection of AI, bias, and social justice

Exploring the intersection of AI, bias, and social justice is crucial in understanding and addressing the ethical implications of AI technologies. Here are key points to consider:

Bias in AI Systems:

AI systems can be influenced by biases present in the data they are trained on. These biases can perpetuate societal inequalities and discriminatory practices. It is important to recognize that AI systems are not inherently neutral but can reflect and amplify existing biases in society.

Impact on Marginalized Communities:

AI bias can disproportionately affect marginalized communities, including racial and ethnic minorities, women, the LGBTQ+ community, and individuals from low-income backgrounds. Biased AI systems can lead to unequal treatment in areas such as criminal justice, employment, healthcare, and financial services.

Discriminatory Outcomes:

AI systems that produce discriminatory outcomes pose ethical concerns. For example, biased algorithms used in hiring processes may perpetuate underrepresentation and perpetuate discriminatory practices. It is essential to critically examine the potential consequences of AI systems and ensure they do not reinforce existing social injustices.

Fairness and Equity:

Promoting fairness and equity in AI systems is a key consideration. This involves ensuring that AI systems are designed and trained to provide equal opportunities and treatment for all individuals, regardless of their demographic characteristics. Fairness should be embedded in the objectives, data, and algorithms used in AI development.

Algorithmic Transparency and Accountability:

Enhancing algorithmic transparency and accountability is

important to address bias in AI systems. Understanding how AI algorithms make decisions and being able to identify and mitigate biases are crucial steps toward ensuring social justice. This includes making AI systems auditable, providing explanations for decisions, and allowing external scrutiny.

Inclusive Data Collection and Representation:

Ensuring inclusive data collection and representation is vital to mitigate bias in AI systems. Diverse datasets that accurately represent the target population can help reduce biases and improve the performance and fairness of AI algorithms. Involving diverse stakeholders in the data collection process and addressing data limitations are important considerations.

Ethical Evaluation and Testing:

Implementing ethical evaluation and testing of AI systems is crucial to identify and mitigate biases. Robust testing frameworks and methodologies can help assess the fairness and equity of AI algorithms, identify potential biases, and inform necessary adjustments and improvements.

Ethical Guidelines and Standards:

Developing and adhering to ethical guidelines and standards for AI development and deployment is essential. These guidelines should address bias, fairness, and social justice considerations. Collaboration between AI researchers, ethicists, policymakers, and affected communities can help establish comprehensive guidelines and standards.

Interdisciplinary Collaboration:

Promoting interdisciplinary collaboration among AI researchers, social scientists, ethicists, and policymakers is key to addressing the intersection of AI, bias, and social justice. Bringing together diverse perspectives can help uncover biases, identify potential harms, and develop strategies for ensuring fairness and social justice in AI systems.

Community Engagement and Participation:

Engaging affected communities in the development and deployment of AI technologies is crucial. Community input, transparency, and accountability can help address concerns, build trust, and ensure that AI systems align with the values and needs of diverse communities.

Exploring the intersection of AI, bias, and social justice requires ongoing research, critical examination, and proactive measures to mitigate bias and promote equitable outcomes. It requires a collective effort to ensure that AI technologies are designed, deployed, and regulated in a manner that upholds social justice principles and safeguards against the perpetuation of biases and inequalities.

Ethical challenges in using AI for decision-making in areas such as criminal justice, healthcare, and resource allocation

The use of AI for decision-making in areas such as

criminal justice, healthcare, and resource allocation presents several ethical challenges. Here are key considerations for each domain:

Criminal Justice:

Bias and Discrimination: AI systems used in criminal justice can inherit biases from historical data, leading to discriminatory outcomes for marginalized communities. The over-policing of certain neighborhoods or racial profiling can be reinforced if not addressed.

Lack of Transparency: The lack of transparency in AI algorithms used for predicting recidivism or determining sentencing can raise concerns about fairness, due process, and the ability to challenge and understand the decisions made by AI systems.

Privacy and Surveillance: The use of AI technologies for surveillance, facial recognition, and predictive policing raises privacy concerns and potential violations of civil liberties.

Accountability and Human Oversight: Ensuring accountability and maintaining human oversight in AI-driven decision-making is crucial to prevent the delegation of decision-making authority solely to machines, as it can lead to the erosion of human rights and the bypassing of legal and ethical safeguards.

Healthcare:

Patient Privacy and Consent: AI systems in healthcare require access to sensitive patient data, raising concerns about privacy, data security, and the potential misuse or unauthorized access to personal health information.

Equity and Access: AI-driven healthcare systems need to ensure equitable access to healthcare services, especially for underserved communities. Failure to address bias in algorithms or disparities in data representation can exacerbate existing healthcare inequities.

Informed Consent and Autonomy: The use of AI for medical diagnosis, treatment recommendation, or decision support should respect patients' autonomy and ensure that individuals are adequately informed about the involvement of AI systems in their care.

Accountability and Liability: Determining the accountability and liability when AI systems are involved in healthcare decision-making can be challenging. Clear guidelines are needed to attribute responsibility in cases of AI-related errors or harm.

Resource Allocation:

Fairness and Distribution: AI algorithms used for resource allocation, such as in welfare programs or disaster relief efforts, must consider fairness, equity, and the needs of vulnerable populations. Ensuring that biases in data or algorithms do not lead to unequal distribution of resources is essential.

Transparency and Explainability: The decision-making processes of AI systems used for resource allocation should be transparent and explainable to instill trust and enable individuals and communities to understand the criteria and reasons behind the allocation decisions.

Ethical Trade-offs: AI-driven resource allocation may require making ethical trade-offs between different individuals or groups. Determining the values and principles that guide these trade-offs is a complex task that should involve public deliberation and inclusive decision-making processes.

Addressing these ethical challenges requires multidisciplinary collaboration, stakeholder engagement, and the integration of ethical considerations into the design, development, and deployment of AI systems. It involves establishing clear guidelines, regulations, and oversight mechanisms to ensure transparency, fairness, accountability, and the protection of human rights in AI-driven decision-making processes.

Ensuring fairness and equity in AI systems to avoid exacerbating existing societal inequalities

Ensuring fairness and equity in AI systems is crucial to prevent the exacerbation of existing societal inequalities. Here are key considerations for promoting fairness and equity:

Diverse and Representative Data:

Ensuring that AI systems are trained on diverse and representative datasets is essential. Datasets should adequately represent the demographics and characteristics of the population the AI system will interact with. This helps mitigate biases and ensures fair treatment across different groups.

Bias Detection and Mitigation:

Implementing mechanisms to detect and address biases in AI systems is important. Regularly assessing the performance of AI algorithms for potential biases and taking corrective actions, such as retraining or adjusting algorithms, can help mitigate unfair outcomes.

Transparency and Explainability:

Promoting transparency in AI systems helps users understand how decisions are made. Providing explanations for AI-generated outcomes can enable individuals to contest unfair decisions and hold accountable the entities responsible for the AI system's development and deployment.

Ethical Guidelines and Standards:

Establishing ethical guidelines and standards specific to fairness and equity in AI development and deployment can guide practitioners and organizations. These guidelines should address issues such as algorithmic bias, discrimination, and the importance of fair treatment across diverse populations.

User Feedback and Participation:

Engaging users and stakeholders affected by AI systems in the design and evaluation processes is crucial. Soliciting feedback and incorporating user perspectives can help identify potential biases, address concerns, and ensure that AI systems align with the values and needs of diverse communities.

Regular Audits and Evaluations:

Conducting regular audits and evaluations of AI systems is important to monitor and assess their fairness and equity. Independent audits and evaluations can help identify biases, measure performance across different groups, and inform necessary improvements and adjustments.

Ethical Considerations in Design:

Integrating ethical considerations, such as fairness and equity, into the design phase of AI systems is essential. It involves incorporating fairness metrics, diverse perspectives, and multidisciplinary collaboration to anticipate and mitigate potential biases before deployment.

Regulatory Frameworks:

Developing regulatory frameworks that promote fairness and equity in AI systems can provide legal protections and accountability. Regulations can address issues such as bias detection and mitigation, transparency requirements, and the impact of AI on marginalized communities.

Continuous Learning and Improvement:

Recognizing that fairness and equity in AI systems are ongoing endeavors. Continuously monitoring, evaluating, and improving AI systems' fairness performance is essential to adapt to evolving societal needs and challenges.

Interdisciplinary Collaboration:

Promoting interdisciplinary collaboration among AI researchers, ethicists, social scientists, policymakers, and affected communities is crucial. Combining diverse expertise and perspectives can help identify biases, address ethical challenges, and ensure the development of AI systems that promote fairness and equity.

By integrating these considerations into AI development and deployment processes, we can strive to create AI systems that are fair, equitable, and contribute to the reduction of existing societal inequalities rather than exacerbating them. It requires a collective effort from various stakeholders to prioritize fairness and equity as fundamental principles in the design and implementation of AI systems.

CHAPTER 9: AI IN WARFARE AND SECURITY

Ethical implications of AI in military applications and autonomous weapons systems

The ethical implications of AI in military applications and autonomous weapons systems are significant and raise important considerations. Here are key points to understand:

Loss of Human Control:

Autonomous weapons systems, equipped with AI, have the potential to operate without direct human control. This raises concerns about the delegation of life-and-death decisions to machines and the potential for uncontrolled escalation of violence.

Accountability and Responsibility:

Determining responsibility and accountability for actions taken by autonomous weapons systems becomes challenging. If AI systems make decisions that result in harm, it may be difficult to attribute blame or seek recourse. This raises questions about legal and ethical accountability.

Lack of Ethical Reasoning:

AI systems lack the ability to comprehend complex ethical considerations, including the principles of proportionality, distinction, and non-combatant immunity. This can lead to ethical dilemmas and violations of humanitarian laws during armed conflicts.

Unintended Consequences:

The deployment of autonomous weapons systems introduces the risk of unintended consequences. The complex nature of AI algorithms and the potential for unpredictable behavior raise concerns about collateral damage, civilian casualties, and the potential for unintended escalation.

Arms Race and Proliferation:

The development and deployment of AI-powered military technologies can trigger an arms race, with nations competing to gain a technological advantage. This can lead to an increased risk of conflict and destabilization, particularly if such technologies fall into the wrong hands.

Ethical Decision-Making:

Ethical considerations should be embedded into the design and use of AI in military applications. This involves ensuring that AI systems are programmed to comply with ethical principles, adhere to international laws and norms, and incorporate human oversight to ensure ethical decision-making.

Humanitarian Impact:

The use of AI in military applications can have significant humanitarian implications. It is important to consider the potential impact on civilians, infrastructure, and the overall conduct of warfare. The proportionality of the use of force and the protection of civilian lives and infrastructure must be upheld.

International Norms and Regulations:

Developing international norms and regulations for the responsible use of AI in military applications is crucial. Multilateral agreements and treaties can establish standards for the development, deployment, and use of autonomous weapons systems, ensuring compliance with ethical and legal frameworks.

Ethical Debate and Public Engagement:

The ethical implications of AI in military applications require public engagement and informed debate. It is essential to involve civil society organizations, ethicists, legal experts, and affected communities to shape the ethical guidelines and policies governing the use of AI in military contexts.

Morally-Driven Technology Development:

Encouraging morally-driven technology development and responsible innovation in military AI can help mitigate the ethical challenges. Adopting a proactive approach that prioritizes human rights, humanitarian considerations, and the prevention of harm is crucial.

Addressing the ethical implications of AI in military applications requires careful consideration, international cooperation, and the integration of ethical guidelines and regulations. Striking a balance between technological advancements and ethical responsibility is essential to ensure that AI technologies in the military domain align with human values, uphold international laws, and minimize harm to civilians.

Considerations surrounding the use of AI for surveillance and cybersecurity

The use of AI for surveillance and cybersecurity introduces several important considerations. Here are key points to understand:

Privacy Concerns:

AI-powered surveillance systems can collect and analyze vast amounts of personal data, raising concerns about privacy infringement. It is crucial to balance the need for security with the protection of individuals' privacy rights and ensure that surveillance measures are proportionate and justified.

Data Security and Protection:

AI systems used for surveillance and cybersecurity rely on sensitive data. Safeguarding this data from unauthorized access, breaches, and misuse is of paramount importance. Robust security measures, encryption, and strict access controls are necessary to protect against cyber threats.

Surveillance State and Civil Liberties:

Widespread use of AI-powered surveillance systems can lead to the creation of a surveillance state, where individuals' movements, activities, and communications are constantly monitored. This raises concerns about the erosion of civil liberties, such as freedom of speech, association, and privacy, if not appropriately regulated and governed.

Bias and Discrimination:

AI algorithms used in surveillance systems can inherit biases from training data, leading to discriminatory outcomes. Bias can disproportionately impact certain individuals or communities, potentially reinforcing existing societal inequalities and perpetuating discrimination.

Transparency and Accountability:

Maintaining transparency and accountability in AI-powered surveillance is crucial. Clear policies and guidelines should be in place to ensure that surveillance practices are governed by law, subject to independent oversight, and accountable to the public.

Ethical Use of Surveillance:

Ethical considerations should guide the use of AI-powered surveillance. This involves deploying surveillance systems for legitimate purposes, ensuring transparency in their deployment, and adhering to legal and ethical guidelines to prevent abuse or misuse.

Cybersecurity Risks:

While AI can enhance cybersecurity defenses, it also introduces new risks. AI systems themselves can be vulnerable to attacks, and malicious actors can exploit AI algorithms or use AI-generated deepfakes to deceive or manipulate systems and individuals.

Dual Use and Weaponization:

AI technologies developed for surveillance and cybersecurity purposes can have dual use capabilities, meaning they can be repurposed for malicious intent.

Safeguarding against the weaponization of AI technologies is crucial to prevent their use in cyberattacks or for unauthorized surveillance.

International Cooperation and Norms:

International cooperation is vital to establish norms, agreements, and frameworks governing the use of AI in surveillance and cybersecurity. Collaborative efforts can help ensure responsible and ethical practices are followed, prevent an unregulated arms race in cyber capabilities, and address transnational cybersecurity threats.

Ethical Oversight and Regulation:

Robust ethical oversight and regulation are necessary to address the ethical considerations of AI in surveillance and cybersecurity. Governments, regulatory bodies, and industry stakeholders should collaborate to establish guidelines, standards, and policies that protect individuals' rights, ensure accountability, and promote the responsible use of AI technologies.

By considering these ethical considerations and implementing appropriate safeguards, it is possible to harness the benefits of AI in surveillance and cybersecurity while upholding individual rights, protecting privacy, and minimizing the potential for abuse or harm. Striking a balance between security and ethical considerations is essential for building public trust and ensuring the responsible use of AI technologies in these domains.

International norms and regulations for governing the development and deployment of AI in warfare

The development and deployment of AI in warfare raise important ethical and legal considerations, leading to discussions on international norms and regulations. Here are key points to consider:

International Humanitarian Law (IHL):

International humanitarian law, also known as the laws of war, provides a legal framework for armed conflict. Existing IHL principles, such as proportionality, distinction, and the prohibition of unnecessary suffering, apply to the use of AI in warfare. These principles aim to protect civilians, limit harm, and maintain a level of humanity in armed conflicts.

Convention on Certain Conventional Weapons (CCW):

The CCW is an international treaty that seeks to regulate or ban specific weapons that may cause excessive harm or have indiscriminate effects. Discussions have taken place under the CCW framework regarding the use of autonomous weapons systems, with efforts to establish guidelines and regulations for their development and deployment.

The Principle of Human Control:

The principle of human control emphasizes that humans should retain ultimate decision-making authority over the use of force. It implies that humans must exercise meaningful control and responsibility in the development, deployment, and operation of AI systems used in warfare.

International Committee of the Red Cross (ICRC) Guidelines:

The ICRC has provided guidance on the use of autonomous weapons systems in armed conflicts. Their guidelines emphasize the importance of compliance with IHL, accountability for harm caused by AI systems, and the need for human control in critical decision-making processes.

United Nations Initiatives:

The United Nations (UN) has been actively engaged in discussions around the use of AI in warfare. The Group of Governmental Experts on Lethal Autonomous Weapons Systems has been meeting under the auspices of the UN to address the ethical, legal, and technical aspects of autonomous weapons. Efforts are being made to establish norms and regulations to govern the development and use of AI in warfare.

Multilateral Treaties and Agreements:

There have been proposals for a legally binding treaty to ban or restrict the use of fully autonomous weapons. The aim is to establish international consensus and obligations to prevent the uncontrolled proliferation and use of AI systems that can operate without meaningful human control.

Ethical Principles and Codes of Conduct:

Various organizations, academic institutions, and industry leaders have proposed ethical principles and codes of conduct for the development and use of AI in warfare. These initiatives aim to guide ethical decision-making, promote transparency, and ensure the responsible and accountable use of AI technologies.

Public Awareness and Engagement:

Public awareness and engagement are crucial in shaping international norms and regulations. Open dialogue, engagement with civil society organizations, and involvement of experts and affected communities can help ensure that ethical considerations and humanitarian concerns are adequately addressed in the development and deployment of AI in warfare.

Compliance and Verification Mechanisms:

Establishing compliance and verification mechanisms can help ensure that nations and actors adhere to international norms and regulations governing AI in warfare. These mechanisms may involve inspections, reporting requirements, and international cooperation to prevent the misuse or proliferation of AI technologies.

Continuing Dialogue and Collaboration:

Continued dialogue, collaboration, and information sharing among nations, experts, and stakeholders are essential for the development of effective international norms and regulations. This ongoing cooperation can help address emerging challenges, consider diverse perspectives, and ensure the responsible development and deployment of AI technologies in the context of warfare.

International norms and regulations for governing AI in warfare are still evolving, with ongoing discussions and initiatives at various levels. The aim is to strike a balance between technological advancements, ethical considerations, and the protection of human rights in armed conflicts.

CHAPTER 10: LOOKING TO THE FUTURE: AI AND ETHICAL PROGRESS

Reflection on the ethical challenges and opportunities presented by AI

Reflection on the ethical challenges and opportunities presented by AI offers insights into the complex and evolving landscape of this technology. Here are some key points to consider:

Ethical Challenges:

Bias and Discrimination: AI systems can perpetuate or amplify biases present in training data, leading to unfair or discriminatory outcomes. Addressing bias and ensuring fairness in AI decision-making is a significant challenge that requires careful consideration and mitigation strategies.

Privacy and Data Protection: The collection, use, and storage of vast amounts of data by AI systems raise concerns about privacy infringement and the potential misuse or unauthorized access to personal information. Safeguarding data and respecting privacy rights are essential ethical considerations.

Lack of Transparency and Explainability: Some AI algorithms, particularly those based on deep learning and complex neural networks, operate as "black boxes" where the decision-making process is not readily explainable. This lack of transparency raises concerns about accountability, trust, and the ability to address potential biases or errors.

Autonomy and Responsibility: Autonomous AI systems raise questions about moral agency, responsibility, and accountability. Determining who is responsible for the actions and decisions of AI systems in various domains poses significant ethical challenges.

Unemployment and Socioeconomic Disparities: The increasing automation of tasks through AI technologies can lead to job displacement and exacerbate socioeconomic disparities. Ensuring a just transition, addressing the impact on workers, and considering the equitable distribution of benefits are ethical imperatives.

Human-AI Interaction and User Consent: As AI systems become more integrated into our daily lives, issues related to human-AI interaction, informed consent, and user autonomy arise. Ethical considerations involve ensuring clear communication, providing understandable explanations, and respecting individuals' choices in their interactions with AI.

Ethical Opportunities:

Enhanced Decision-Making: AI has the potential to augment human decision-making processes, providing more accurate and efficient insights. This can be particularly beneficial in areas such as healthcare, finance, and scientific research.

Efficiency and Productivity: AI technologies can streamline processes, automate repetitive tasks, and increase efficiency in various sectors. This has the potential to free up human resources for more creative and value-added endeavors.

Accessibility and Inclusion: AI can contribute to creating more inclusive and accessible environments by enabling personalized experiences, providing assistive technologies, and addressing barriers for individuals with disabilities.

Scientific Advancement and Innovation: AI is driving significant scientific advancements, fueling breakthroughs in fields such as medicine, climate science, and astronomy. These advancements offer opportunities to tackle pressing societal challenges and improve quality of life.

Humanitarian Applications: AI has the potential to be leveraged for humanitarian purposes, including disaster response, healthcare in underserved areas, and addressing societal inequalities. Ethical considerations involve ensuring these applications prioritize human well-being and adhere to human rights principles.

Sustainable Development: AI can contribute to achieving sustainable development goals by optimizing resource allocation, improving energy efficiency, and facilitating smarter urban planning. Ethical considerations involve using AI technologies in ways that prioritize environmental sustainability and social responsibility.

Reflecting on these ethical challenges and opportunities allows us to navigate the development and deployment of AI in a responsible and ethical manner. It emphasizes the need for ongoing dialogue, interdisciplinary collaboration, and the involvement of diverse stakeholders to shape the future of AI in a way that aligns with societal values and promotes the well-being of humanity.

Promoting responsible AI development and adoption

Promoting responsible AI development and adoption is crucial to ensure that AI technologies are developed and deployed in an ethical, inclusive, and beneficial manner. Here are some key strategies and considerations for promoting responsible AI:

Ethical Guidelines and Principles: Develop and adhere to ethical guidelines and principles that govern AI development and use. These guidelines should encompass principles such as fairness, transparency, accountability, privacy, and avoiding harm. They should be developed in collaboration with experts, stakeholders, and impacted communities.

Interdisciplinary Collaboration: Foster interdisciplinary collaboration between AI researchers, ethicists, policymakers, social scientists, and other relevant stakeholders. This collaboration can help ensure that ethical considerations are integrated into the development process and that the societal implications of AI are adequately addressed.

Diversity and Inclusion: Promote diversity and inclusion in AI development teams to avoid bias and ensure that different perspectives and experiences are considered. Diverse teams are more likely to identify potential biases and ethical issues that may otherwise be overlooked.

Ethical Review Processes: Implement robust ethical review processes to assess AI systems before deployment. This includes evaluating potential biases, privacy concerns, and potential impacts on vulnerable populations. Ethical review boards can provide guidance and oversight to ensure responsible AI development.

Data Governance and Privacy: Establish strong data governance frameworks that prioritize privacy, consent, and data protection. Develop mechanisms to ensure that data used in AI systems is obtained ethically, and that individuals have control over their personal data.

Transparency and Explainability: Promote transparency and explainability in AI systems, especially when they are used in critical decision-making processes. Users and stakeholders should be able to understand how AI systems arrive at their decisions and have access to meaningful explanations.

Continuous Monitoring and Evaluation: Implement ongoing monitoring and evaluation of AI systems to identify and address any biases or unintended consequences that may arise during deployment. Regular audits and assessments can help identify and rectify ethical issues.

Public Awareness and Education: Educate the public about AI technologies, their benefits, and potential risks. Promote awareness of ethical considerations, privacy concerns, and the societal impact of AI. Empower individuals to make informed decisions about AI adoption and engage in discussions about its responsible development.

Regulatory Frameworks: Develop and enforce appropriate regulations and standards to govern AI development and deployment. These regulations should address ethical concerns, protect individual rights, and ensure that AI technologies adhere to ethical guidelines and principles.

Collaboration with Industry: Foster collaboration with industry leaders to establish ethical standards, share best practices, and promote responsible AI development. Encourage industry self-regulation and engagement with ethical considerations.

International Cooperation: Foster international cooperation and collaboration to establish global norms and regulations for responsible AI development and adoption. Engage in discussions and initiatives at the international level to ensure ethical considerations are addressed globally.

Promoting responsible AI development and adoption requires a collective effort from researchers, policymakers, industry leaders, civil society organizations, and the public. By prioritizing ethical considerations and following these strategies, we can harness the potential of AI while ensuring it aligns with societal values, benefits all individuals, and avoids harmful consequences.

Speculating on the future of AI ethics and potential ethical advancements

Speculating on the future of AI ethics involves envisioning the potential ethical advancements and challenges that may emerge as AI continues to evolve. While the future is uncertain, here are some areas to consider:

Enhanced Ethical Frameworks: Ethical frameworks specific to AI may continue to evolve and become more refined. As AI systems become more complex and integrated into various aspects of society, ethical considerations may need to be adapted and expanded to address new challenges and dilemmas.

Ethical AI Design: The concept of ethical design may gain prominence, focusing on integrating ethical considerations into the design and development of AI systems from the outset. Ethical design principles could guide the creation of AI technologies that prioritize fairness, transparency, accountability, and societal well-being.

Value Alignment: Advancements may be made in aligning AI systems with human values and preferences. Researchers may explore methods to better understand and incorporate diverse human values into AI systems, ensuring that they reflect the values and priorities of the individuals and communities they interact with.

Explainable AI: Efforts may continue to develop more explainable AI systems, enabling better understanding of the decision-making process. This could involve research into techniques and algorithms that provide interpretable explanations for AI decisions, improving transparency and accountability.

AI Governance and Regulation: The development of comprehensive governance frameworks and regulations specific to AI may become more prevalent. Governments and international bodies may work together to establish standards and guidelines that ensure responsible AI development, deployment, and use.

Ethical Auditing and Certification: Ethical auditing and certification processes for AI systems may be established to assess compliance with ethical principles and guidelines. Similar to security audits, ethical audits could evaluate the fairness, transparency, and impact of AI systems on different stakeholders.

Human-in-the-Loop Systems: Human-in-the-loop approaches may be further explored to balance the benefits of AI with human oversight and control. Ensuring that humans remain engaged in decision-making processes and have the ability to intervene when necessary can help address ethical concerns and mitigate risks.

Ethical Training for AI Practitioners: The inclusion of ethics training in AI education and training programs may become more widespread. AI practitioners could be equipped with a deeper understanding of ethical considerations and trained to apply ethical frameworks throughout the AI development lifecycle.

Global Collaboration: International collaboration on AI ethics may expand, fostering knowledge sharing, policy alignment, and best practices. Collaborative efforts can help address the ethical challenges of AI in a global context, promoting consistency and ensuring shared responsibility.

Public Engagement and Participation: Increased public engagement and participation in shaping AI ethics may become a norm. Public consultation, citizen assemblies, and participatory approaches could allow individuals to have a say in the development and deployment of AI systems, ensuring that their values and concerns are considered.

It is important to note that these speculations represent potential directions and are subject to various factors, including technological advancements, social dynamics, and regulatory frameworks. The future of AI ethics will depend on the collective efforts of researchers, policymakers, industry leaders, and society as a whole to shape the ethical development and deployment of AI technologies.

CONCLUSION

Recap of key ethical considerations in the field of AI

In the field of AI, there are several key ethical considerations that need to be addressed. Here is a recap of some of these considerations:

Bias and Fairness: AI systems can inherit biases from training data, leading to unfair outcomes. Ensuring fairness and addressing bias in AI algorithms and datasets is crucial to avoid perpetuating discrimination and inequities.

Privacy and Data Protection: The collection, use, and storage of data in AI raise ethical concerns regarding privacy. Safeguarding personal information, obtaining informed consent, and implementing robust data protection measures are essential.

Transparency and Explainability: AI systems should be transparent and provide explanations for their decision-making processes. Understanding how AI arrives at its conclusions promotes accountability and helps identify potential biases or errors.

Accountability: AI systems must be designed with mechanisms for accountability. Identifying responsible parties, establishing clear lines of responsibility, and addressing potential negative impacts are vital for ensuring accountability in AI decision-making.

Human Autonomy and Control: AI systems should respect and uphold human autonomy and control. Humans should have the ability to understand and override AI decisions, especially in areas with significant ethical implications.

Beneficence and Non-Maleficence: AI systems should aim to maximize benefits while minimizing harm. Designing AI technologies that prioritize human well-being and avoiding adverse consequences is essential.

Social and Economic Impact: AI has the potential to disrupt employment and exacerbate societal inequalities. Ethical considerations include ensuring fair distribution of benefits, supporting re-skilling and job transition programs, and avoiding detrimental impacts on marginalized communities.

Ethical Governance and Regulation: Establishing

effective governance mechanisms and regulatory frameworks is necessary to ensure ethical AI development, deployment, and use. These frameworks should be adaptable, transparent, and capable of keeping pace with technological advancements.

Inclusivity and Diversity: Promoting inclusivity and diversity in AI development teams helps mitigate biases and ensures that AI systems consider a wide range of perspectives and experiences.

Ethical Research and Testing: Conducting ethical research and testing of AI systems involves minimizing potential risks, obtaining informed consent from participants, and ensuring the ethical treatment of data and subjects.

These considerations highlight the need for a comprehensive and interdisciplinary approach to AI ethics, involving collaboration between researchers, policymakers, industry leaders, ethicists, and the public. By addressing these ethical considerations, we can work towards the responsible development and deployment of AI technologies that align with societal values, benefit all individuals, and avoid harmful consequences.

Call to action for stakeholders to prioritize ethics in AI development and deployment

The call to action for stakeholders to prioritize ethics in AI development and deployment is essential to ensure that AI technologies are developed and utilized responsibly. Here are some key points for stakeholders to consider:

Ethical Leadership: Leaders in the field of AI, including researchers, industry executives, and policymakers, should prioritize ethics as a fundamental aspect of AI development. They should set an example by integrating ethical considerations into their decision-making processes and advocating for responsible AI practices.

Education and Awareness: Stakeholders should promote education and awareness about AI ethics among AI practitioners, policymakers, and the general public. This includes providing resources, training programs, and workshops to foster understanding and engagement with ethical principles in AI.

Collaboration and Interdisciplinary Dialogue: Stakeholders should foster collaboration and interdisciplinary dialogue among researchers, ethicists, policymakers, industry representatives, and affected communities. Engaging in open and inclusive discussions allows for a broader perspective on ethical issues and ensures that diverse viewpoints are considered.

Ethical Guidelines and Frameworks: Development and adoption of ethical guidelines and frameworks specific to AI should be encouraged. These guidelines should address key ethical considerations and provide practical guidance for developers and users of AI systems.

Ethical Impact Assessments: Stakeholders should conduct ethical impact assessments to evaluate the potential ethical implications of AI systems before their deployment. These assessments can help identify and mitigate any ethical risks and challenges associated with AI technologies.

Responsible Data Practices: Stakeholders should prioritize responsible data practices, including the collection, storage, and use of data in AI systems. This involves obtaining informed consent, ensuring data privacy and security, and mitigating biases and discrimination in data sets.

Public Engagement and Participation: Engaging the public in AI decision-making processes is crucial. Stakeholders should seek public input, involve affected communities, and consider diverse perspectives to ensure that AI technologies align with societal values and priorities.

Regulatory Frameworks: Policymakers and regulators should develop and enforce appropriate regulations and standards for AI development and deployment. These frameworks should address ethical considerations, protect individual rights, and ensure accountability and transparency.

Ethical Auditing and Certification: Establishing mechanisms for ethical auditing and certification of AI systems can provide independent verification of adherence to ethical guidelines and principles. Stakeholders should support the development of auditing and certification processes to promote responsible AI practices.

Continuous Evaluation and Improvement: Stakeholders should continuously evaluate and improve AI systems to address emerging ethical challenges and ensure that ethical standards are met. This involves monitoring the impact of AI technologies, gathering feedback, and iteratively refining practices to align with evolving ethical norms.

By prioritizing ethics in AI development and deployment, stakeholders can help shape the future of AI in a manner that is inclusive, accountable, and beneficial to society as a whole. It is a collective responsibility to ensure that AI technologies align with human values, respect individual rights, and contribute positively to the well-being of individuals and communities.

Encouragement for ongoing dialogue and interdisciplinary collaboration to shape the future of AI and ethics

Encouraging ongoing dialogue and interdisciplinary collaboration is crucial for shaping the future of AI and ethics. Here's why such collaboration is essential:

Complex Ethical Challenges: The intersection of AI and ethics presents complex and multifaceted challenges that require diverse perspectives and expertise. Bringing together professionals from fields such as technology, ethics, law, sociology, philosophy, and policymaking fosters a comprehensive understanding of the ethical implications of AI.

Holistic Approach: Collaborative dialogue ensures a holistic approach to addressing AI's ethical concerns. By engaging in interdisciplinary discussions, stakeholders can explore the broader societal impacts, cultural considerations, and long-term consequences of AI technologies, leading to more well-rounded ethical frameworks.

Identifying Blind Spots: Different disciplines bring unique insights to the table, enabling the identification of blind spots and potential biases in AI systems and ethical frameworks. By actively seeking perspectives from multiple fields, stakeholders can uncover unintended consequences, uncover hidden biases, and make more informed decisions.

Ethical Innovation: Collaboration between AI researchers, ethicists, and practitioners encourages the development of innovative solutions to ethical challenges. By combining technical expertise with ethical insights, stakeholders can design AI systems that embed ethical principles from the early stages of development, leading to responsible and beneficial outcomes.

Public Engagement: Interdisciplinary collaboration enables meaningful public engagement and involvement in shaping AI ethics. Including diverse voices, perspectives, and experiences ensures that ethical frameworks and AI policies align with societal values and address the concerns of those directly affected by AI technologies.

Agile Response to Ethical Issues: Ongoing dialogue and collaboration allow for an agile response to emerging ethical issues in AI. As AI evolves, new ethical challenges will arise. By maintaining open channels of communication and collaboration, stakeholders can adapt ethical frameworks, policies, and regulations to address these emerging concerns effectively.

Shared Responsibility: The ethical implications of AI extend beyond individual stakeholders or disciplines. Collaboration ensures shared responsibility, fostering a collective effort to address ethical challenges and create a more inclusive and responsible AI ecosystem.

Ethical Standardization: Interdisciplinary collaboration can contribute to the development of ethical standards and best practices for AI. Consensus-building and collective deliberation lead to the establishment of common principles and guidelines that promote responsible AI development, deployment, and use.

Ethical Governance: Dialogue and collaboration facilitate the development of effective ethical governance mechanisms for AI. By bringing together experts and stakeholders, policymakers can design regulations and policies that strike a balance between innovation, ethical considerations, and societal values.

Continuous Learning and Improvement: Ongoing dialogue ensures a continuous learning process, where stakeholders can share experiences, insights, and lessons learned. This iterative approach fosters continuous improvement in AI ethics, allowing for the refinement and evolution of ethical frameworks in response to new challenges and opportunities.

By fostering ongoing dialogue and interdisciplinary collaboration, stakeholders can collectively address the ethical implications of AI, shape responsible practices, and contribute to the development of AI technologies that align with human values, societal needs, and the broader public interest.

ABOUT THE AUTHOR

Sales and Marketing Professional with more than 25 Plus years of diversified experience for both transnational and national pharmaceutical companies such as Merck & Co. Inc. NV Organon, AkzoNobel, and OBS Pakistan (Pvt.) Limited. Moreover, he is a university Professor and has more than 10 years' experience of teaching, research and supervising dissertations for MBA, MS. M.Phil., and Ph.D. level students. He is an author and coauthor of more than 200 publications, in which he has written more than 80 impact factor research articles, and 20 books.